Cover illustration: Following all the various ad-hoc camouflage schemes initiated since the Falklands conflict, post-Falklands Sea Harriers are to be finished in an overall dark sea-grey scheme, with 'B'-type roundels and black serial numbers and squadron markings. This photograph, taken in January 1983, shows three representative Sea Harrier FRS.1s from 800 Naval Air Squadron (NAS), 801 NAS and 899 NAS. Note that the 899 NAS aircraft still has medium sea-grey gun pods and underwing tanks, from an unpainted 809 NAS aircraft. (Nigel B. Thomas, HMS *Heron*)

1. Because of systems incompatibility, RAF Harriers could not use their 68mm SNEB rocket system from *Hermes* during the Falklands War, and so in April 1982 Gr.3s were modified to use the Navy's 2in rocket pods, as illustrated in this photograph. (RAF Wittering)

WARBIRDS ILLUSTRATED NO. 20

HARRIER

MICHAEL J. GETHING

ARMS AND ARMOUR PRESS
London – Melbourne – Harrisburg. Pa. – Cape Town

Introduction

Warbirds Illustrated 20: Harrier
Published in 1983 by
Arms and Armour Press, Lionel Leventhal
Limited, 2–6 Hampstead High Street, London
NW3 1QQ; 4–12 Tattersalls Lane, Melbourne,
Victoria 3000, Australia; Sanso Centre, 8 Adderley
Street, P.O. Box 94, Cape Town 8000, South
Africa; Cameron and Kelker Streets, P.O. Box
1831, Harrisburg, Pennsylvania 17105, USA

Layout by Roger Chesneau.
Typesetting and make-up by
Wyvern Typesetting Limited, Bristol.
Printed and bound in Great Britain by
William Clowes, Beccles, Limited.

If any proof regarding the ability of the Harrier/Sea Harrier family to be able to operate successfully in a hostile combat environment were needed, the events in the South Atlantic during the spring and summer of 1982 supplied that proof. The official claims for Sea Harrier kills, amended slightly for the post-Falkland White Paper, puts AIM-9 Sidewinder kills at 16 (plus one probable) and 30mm gunfire kills at four (plus two probables). The world's only operational V/STOL combat aircraft had won its spurs.

The concept of vertical take-off has been tried in many formats in the Western aviation industry since the mid-1950s, but to date only the vectored-thrust Harrier and the Soviet Yak-36 Forger (with twin lift jets forward and a twin-nozzle vectored rear engine) have succeeded. While both types are pure VTOL, only the Harrier has the ability to make short take-offs and landings. Indeed, operationally, both Harriers and Sea Harriers use the short take-off, vertical landing (STOVL) mode. Even the United States has had to take the attitude 'If you can't beat 'em, join 'em'. After their first taste of Harriers (in AV-8A form), however, McDonnell Douglas has refined the aerodynamics of the AV-8A to produce the AV-8B, but the powerplant, without which none of the Harrier progenitors or successors could have flown, remains the Pegasus vectored-thrust turbofan, which will be procured from Rolls-Royce.

Therein lies the crux of the Harrier's success. Through P.1127, Kestrel, P.1154, Harrier, AV-8A, AV-16, Sea Harrier, AV-8B and beyond, the one common factor is the Pegasus powerplant. Within the pages of this book, you can see all the external shapes which have surrounded that engine, and the shape is basically the same, refined only by changes in aerodynamics. In one form or another, the Harrier has been around for twenty-three years, and I feel sure that it will still be in the skies in the year 2000.

In compiling this collection of Harrier photographs I am indebted to the 'Two Johns' at British Aerospace (BAe) Kingston, Messrs Combes and Godden; to Geoff Norris and Karen Stubberfield at McDonnell Douglas; Dick Butcher at Rolls-Royce, Bristol; Lieutenant-Commander Jan Larkham at HMS *Heron*, Flight-Lieutenant John Blenkieron at RAF Wittering; Dick Ward of Modeldecal; Richard E. Gardner of *RAF News*; and the press pictures facility at MoD Main Building. I even managed to include several shots from my own collection. Together the photographs cover the whole spectrum of the Harrier to date.

Michael J. Gething, Farnborough, 1983.

2. A Sea Harrier FRS.1 of 809 NAS landing aboard HMS *Invincible* after a combat patrol during the Falklands conflict. (Via BAe Kingston)

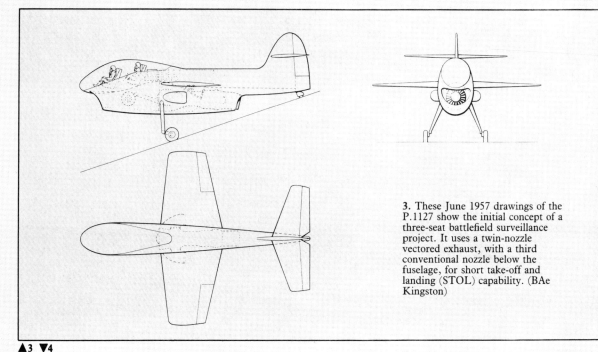

3. These June 1957 drawings of the
P.1127 show the initial concept of a
three-seat battlefield surveillance
project. It uses a twin-nozzle
vectored exhaust, with a third
conventional nozzle below the
fuselage, for short take-off and
landing (STOL) capability. (BAe
Kingston)

▲3 ▼4

4. Development of the vertical take-off and landing (VTOL)
concept was begun by Hawkers' Sir Sydney Camm in 1957,
following the infamous Sandys Defence White Paper foretelling
the end of the manned interceptor fighter (sic). This
photograph shows the resulting private venture prototype,
P.1127, during its second tethered hover over the grid at
Dunsfold in October 1960. (BAe Kingston)

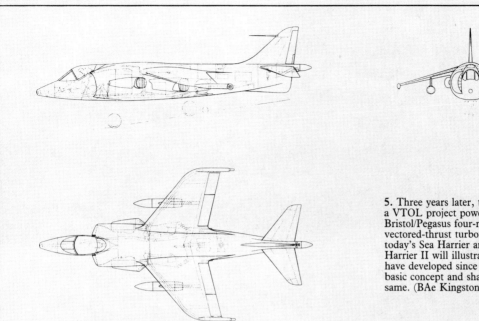

5. Three years later, the P.1127 was a VTOL project powered by the Bristol/Pegasus four-nozzle vectored-thrust turbofan. A look at today's Sea Harrier and AV-8B Harrier II will illustrate how things have developed since 1960. The basic concept and shape remain the same. (BAe Kingston)

▲6

▲7 ▼8

6. By November 1960, the P.1127, serial number XP831, was performing untethered hovers from Dunsfold, and some minor problems found during tethered flight were resolved with the removal of the tethers. Note the bell-shaped air intake lips and the ground-air communications link trailing from the starboard outrigger wheel. In the interest of saving weight, radio had not yet been fitted. (BAe Kingston)

7. The second prototype P.1127 during flight trials. Note the long nose probe, and outrigger wheel fairings which extend beyond the leading edge of the wing. (BAe Kingston)

8. The fifth prototype – XP980 – making a vertical landing at Dunsfold. First flown in May 1963, it was still making a contribution to Harrier development at RAF Gaydon in 1973. (BAe Kingston)

9. The third prototype – XP972 – was the first of four Ministry of Aviation-sponsored development aircraft. It first flew in April 1962, and featured low-profile air intake lips and faired-in outrigger pylons. This aircraft was lost on 30 October 1962 during a forced landing at RAF Tangmere, following an engine failure in the air, and an undercarriage failure on the ground. The pilot, Hugh Merewether, escaped unhurt. (BAe Kingston)

10. From the P.1127 was developed the Kestrel FGA.1, of which nine aircraft were ordered for a Tripartite Evaluation unit from the Central Fighter Establishment. Based at West Raynham from 1964–65, the unit consisted of pilots and groundcrew from the RAF, USAF, US Navy (but curiously, not the US Marine Corps), US Army and Luftwaffe. Illustrated here is the fourth Kestrel – XS691 – taxiing at West Raynham, with another of the type hovering in the background. (BAe Kingston)

10▼ 9▲

▲11 ▼12

11. This view shows the second Kestrel – XS689 – and the eighth – XS695 – during a sortie from West Raynham. XS689 later became one of the six Kestrels shipped to the United States after the end of the evaluation, where they were designated XV-6A for Tri-Service Evaluation at the US Navy Test Centre at Patuxent River, Maryland.

12. Seven of the nine Tripartite Kestrels on the grounds at West Raynham. During the evaluation, some 938 sorties, totalling some 600 hours were flown by the pilots of Britain, Germany and America. Their brief was to assess the practical merits and difficulties of jet V/STOL operations. (BAe Kingston)

13▲ 14▼

13. Even as the Tripartite evaluation was being planned, the RAF and Royal Navy were brought together to consider a supersonic V/STOL project. During 1962 work began on the P.1154, to be powered by the Bristol Siddeley BS.100 with plenum chamber burning (PCB), the vectored-thrust equivalent of afterburning. This model shows the P.1154/RAF version with single cockpit and P.1127 outrigger wheels. This version had supersonic dash capability and a sophisticated terrain-following radar. (BAe Kingston)

14. The Royal Navy version, the P.1154/RN, as illustrated by this model, was to have been a two-man carrier-borne interceptor armed with advanced AAMs and possessing a sustained supersonic (Mach 2.5) capability. To enable the outer wing panels to fold (for carrier stowage), the undercarriage was reconfigured from the bicycle/outrigger system of the P.1127 to conventional nose and main wheels (the latter being housed in fairings in the centre of the trailing edge of the wing). By 1964, the Royal Navy opted out of the project, preferring to go for the McDonnell Douglas F-4K Phantom and leaving the RAF with a more expensive programme as a result. The axe fell with the appointment of Denis Healey as Minister of Defence on 2 January 1965, and the P.1154/RAF was cancelled on 2 February of that year. (BAe Kingston)

▲15

▲16 ▼17

18▲ 19▼

15. Following the cancellation of the P.1154, a developed version of the Kestrel was ordered for the RAF. The P.1127 (RAF), later christened the Harrier, was swiftly produced to RAF Air Staff Requirement (ASR) 384, but it was to be firmly subsonic in level flight. Six pre-production Harrier GR.1s were ordered, the first of which flew in August 1966. This photograph shows the fourth development batch aircraft – XV279 – with a 1,000lb bomb in the foreground, and two pairs of drop tanks (of 230- and 100-gallon capacity respectively) and a pair of SNEB rocket pods in the background. (BAe Kingston)

16. The last of the six development (pre-production) batch of Harrier GR.1s ('G' for ground attack, 'R' for reconnaissance) on a flight from Dunsfold. It was practically fully representative of the production Harrier, with the eight blow-in doors on the air-intake side, used to provide a greater airflow to the Pegasus 6 turbofan engine. (BAe Kingston)

17. The first RAF unit to receive the Harrier GR.1 was 1 Squadron, based at RAF Wittering, who received their first aircraft on 18 April 1969. The Harrier Conversion Unit, later redesignated 233 Operational Conversion Unit (OCU) was formed at Wittering early in 1970. This photograph shows one of the first 1 Squadron Harrier Gr.1s with only the squadron badge above the fin flash to indicate its affiliation. (BAe Kingston)

18. Harrier GR.1 – XV744 – takes-off from a coalyard next to St. Pancras station in London at the start of the Daily Mail London-to-New York Air Race in 1969. (BAe Kingston)

19. Harrier GR.1 landing at Bristol Basin, Manhattan in New York, on the last leg of the air race in 1969. The Harriers, configured with 100-gallon tanks and in-flight refuelling probes, were refuelled by RAF Victor tankers *en route*. (BAe Kingston)

20. This photograph shows a formation of four Harrier GR.1s over the ranges, configured with SNEB rocket pods on the inner pylons and CBLS on the outer pylons. Note that the red-white-blue 'D'-type roundels have been replaced by red-blue 'B'-type roundels, reverting to the low-visibility markings of the Second World War. (BAe Kingston)

21. No. 1 Squadron adopted both the badge over the fin flash and a nose insignia to indicate ownership. This aircraft – XV745 – was delivered in August 1969, and was later converted to GR.3 configuration. (Via RAF Wittering)

22. Operations in the field, flying from dispersed sites soon became the rule rather than the exception for the Harrier units. Here a Harrier Gr.1 of 1 Squadron undergoes routine maintenance in an inflatable hangar. (RAF).

23. During the early 1970s, the Pegasus 10 engine, delivering 20,000lb of thrust, was retrofitted to the GR.1, which became the GR.1A. There was no external difference in appearance in the aircraft. Here a GR.1A of 3 Squadron, usually based (at that time) at RAF Wildenrath in Germany, is seen operating from a dispersed site in Germany during Exercise 'Oak Stroll' in June 1974. Note the aircraft 'hides' at the edge of the woods below the airborne Harrier. (RAF Germany).

24. A Harrier GR.1A of 20 Squadron being towed to its hide by an Eager Beaver rough terrain fork-lift truck during Exercise 'Grimm Charade' in the Westphalia region of Germany during August 1975. The pilot is climbing out of the cockpit; the under-fuselage gun pods are clearly visible. (RAF Germany)

25. The fifth prototype Hawker P.1127 during development trials at Hawker's Dunsfold airfield in 1963. Note the partially inflated bag-type air intake lips being used at that time. (BAe Kingston)

26. The British Aerospace demonstrator aircraft, a two-seat Harrier T.52, appropriately registered G-VTOL, takes off from the ski-jump launch ramp set at a 15° exit angle at RAE Bedford on 14 April 1978. (BAe Kingston)

▲23 ▼24

▲27 ▼28

27. An AV-8A Harrier of VMA-231 making a vertical landing on one of the US Navy's amphibious assault ships. Note the older-style 'stars 'n' bars' insignia. (Rolls-Royce, Leavesden)

28. A US Marine Corps (USMC) AV-8A Harrier of VMA-231 on board a *Tarawa*-class amphibious assault ship (LHA) during an exercise deployment. (BAe Kingston)

29. Another view of a 20 Squadron Harrier GR.1A, this time during Exercise 'Heath Fir' in June 1976. The aircraft is taking off from a short strip at a dispersed site. The RAF prefer to use their Harriers in the STOVL mode (Short Take-off, Vertical Landing) to allow greater take-off weights associated with the short take-off. (Corporal Bob Clarke, RAF Germany)

30. Disguised under a hide, near an airfield perimeter rests a Harrier GR.1A of 233 OCU, armed with cannon and two SNEB pods. Note the aluminium planking laid on the grass for the aircraft. The bicycle-type main undercarriage is clearly visible. (MoD)

29▲ 30▼

▲31 ▼32

▼33

31. Between 1973 and 1976, the RAF's Harrier fleet was upgraded from GR.1A to GR.3 standard. The modification consisted of three improvements, and this photograph clearly shows the first. Sometimes known as 'the bodger on the bonce', this 1 Squadron Harrier GR.3 features the Ferranti Laser Ranger and Marked Target Seeker (LRMTS) in a new lengthened nose. This system enables the pilot to provide ranging data from laser pulses originating in the LRMTS, or alternatively, it can seek laser emissions from a target designated by a Forward Air Controller marking the target from the ground with a laser designator. (Ian V. Hogg)

32. The final improvement for the GR.3, not externally visible, is the new Pegasus 11 turbofan engine, featuring a re-fanned blade which increases its thrust to 21,500lb. This 1 Squadron aircraft also shows the RWR and LRMTS to its advantage, as well as the arctic camouflage. (Rolls-Royce, Leavesden)

33. Framed by the wing of an RAF Hercules C.1, this 1 Squadron Harrier GR.3 is towed to its dispersal point on Tromso airfield during Exercise 'Anorak Express' in March 1980. The second improvement for the GR.3 can be seen on the leading edge of the fin, near the tip, and on the end of the tailcone. These are the two antennae which comprise the radar warning receiver (RWR) system, which tells the pilot if he is being 'painted' by an enemy radar. (Ian V. Hogg)

20

34. This photograph provides an interesting comparison between the Harrier GR.3 (nearest the camera) and the GR.1A. Both aircraft belong to 3 Squadron, now based at RAF Gutersloh in Germany, the only RAF airfield east of the Rhine. (BAe Kingston).

35. Three Harrier GR.3s of 3 Squadron, based at RAF Gutersloh in Germany, on a training flight. The aircraft are carrying twin 30mm Aden cannon pods under the fuselage, with a CBLS (Carrier, Bombs, Light Stores) unit on the centre fuselage hardpoint, and two 100-gallon drop tanks on the inner hardpoints. (BAe Kingston)

34▲ 35▼

▲36 ▼37

▼38

22

36. Another view of a 3 Squadron Harrier GR.3 taking-off from a short strip during Exercise 'Heath Fir' in the Borken area of Germany in June 1976. (Corporal Bob Clarke, RAF Germany)
37. Although these two Harriers appear to be GR.1As, they are, in fact, GR.3s, prior to having the RWR and LRMTS equipment fitted. This photograph, dated November 1976, was issued by RAF Germany to commemorate the first two pilots in Germany to notch up their 1,000 hours on the Harrier. Flight-Lieutenants Dave Linney and Kit Adams were both serving with 4 Squadron at the time. (Barry Ellson)
38. This photograph of a 4 Squadron Harrier GR.3, taken in July 1981, shows the aircraft in the overall grey/green

camouflage adopted in the late 1970s, spreading the upper surface camouflage onto the undersides of the aircraft to enhance its survivability at low levels. (MJG)
39. Another view of a 4 Squadron Harrier GR.3, which clearly shows the hardened aircraft shelters built on the German bases to protect the aircraft from all but a direct hit. Each HAS, as they are known, can accommodate three Harriers at a pinch, but more usually operate with two. (MJG)
40. Despite the availability of the HAS, the German Harrier Wing expects to go to war from dispersed sites. Here a Unimog truck positions a 4 Squadron Harrier GR.3 in a hide during a practice deployment in 1981. (RAF Germany)

41. Inside the 'office', the nozzle-vectoring lever can be seen fully forward (down) with the throttle on its left, closed. The Smith's Industries head-up display (HUD) can be seen immediately behind the windscreen, with a padded 'bumper' below. The screen in the centre of the instrument panel, behind the control column is where the moving-map display, fed by the Ferranti inertial navigation/attack system, is located. To the left of the moving-map screen are the armament switches. (Smith's Industries)

42. This 233 OCU Harrier GR.3, seen at RAF Lyneham during Exercise 'Avon Express' in 1977, has the 'wrap-around' camouflage scheme now common to all RAF Harriers. Note that the under-fuselage airbrake is lowered when parked on the ground. (MJG)

43. Easy does it! A Harrier wing is lifted from a GR.1A to facilitate an engine change in the field, under the shelter of an inflatable hangar during Exercise 'Heath Fir' in June 1976. (RAF Germany)

▲41 ▼42

44. Spot the Harrier! A fully camouflaged dispersed hide adjacent to a spinney and a ploughed field provides the perfect hiding-place for a Harrier and crew near the forward edge of the battle area. (BAe Kingston)

43▲ 44▼

45. Although there were proposals for a two-seat P.1127, it was not until 1966 that a contract was placed for a two-seat Harrier. This photograph shows the company demonstration aircraft, designated the T.52, in its initial red, white and blue colour scheme. The aircraft features the 18in fin extension, retro-fitted to early trainers which were built with the shorter fin. Registered as G-VTOL, this aircraft first flew in September 1971. (BAe Kingston)

46. The first production two-seat Harrier T.2 with the original fin profile. First flown in October 1969, it was preceded by two development aircraft. This Harrier is armed with two Hunting BL755 cluster bombs on the outer pylons, three 1,000lb HE bombs on the inner and centre pylons plus two 30mm Aden cannon. (BAe Kingston)

47. This Harrier two-seater was delivered as a T.2A (with the Pegasus 10 of the GR.1A), and was later brought up to T.4 standard with the Pegasus 11. Delivered to 233 OCU, it sports the nose markings initially applied, which consist of the words 'Harrier Operational' above a grasshopper and 'Conversion Unit' below the grasshopper. (BAe Kingston)

48. This photograph clearly shows the raised and lengthened forward fuselage of the Harrier T.2, this example of which has been built with the taller fin. Note the two under-fuselage strakes in place of the Aden gun pods. (BAe Kingston)

▲45 ▼46

▼47

48▶

49. A Harrier T.4 of 1 Squadron at RAF Wittering under a mobile floodlight while preparing for night flying. Note the sideways hinging double canopy of the type. (Simplon)

50. The latest colour scheme for G-VTOL, the British Aerospace T.52 demonstration, is light aircraft grey with white undersides, as depicted in this photograph. The Harrier also carries the military serial ZA250, as required by law to enable it to engage in weapon-firing trials. BAe Hawk demonstrator G-HAWK/ZA101 flies in company with G-VTOL. (BAe Kingston)

51. This photograph shows a Harrier T.4 of 4 Squadron based at RAF Gutersloh in July 1981, complete with LRMTS and RWR. (MJG)

52. During the 1980 Farnborough Air Show, the author was fortunate enough to experience two take-offs from the ski-jump ramp in the back seat of G-VTOL. Although totally unrecognizable, he is in the back seat of the aircraft in this picture. (R. L. Ward)

◀49 ▲50

51▲ 52▼

53. The US Marine Corps (USMC) provided the Harrier with its first export order when, in the FY 1970 US Defense Budget, 12 AV-8A Harriers were funded. Later 102 AV-8As were to be procured. This photograph shows a USMC aircraft taking off from a dusty Savannah road during deployment exercises. Note the flight-refuelling probe, which is a 'bolt-on' modification to all Harriers. (BAe Kingston)

54. Although the USMC purchase of Harriers was 'off-the-shelf', some minor modifications were made to the AV-8A. One of these was the provision for AIM-9 Sidewinder AAM on the outer pylons, as illustrated by this aircraft of VMA-513. (BAe Kingston)

▲53 ▼54

55. An early 1970s view of four AV-8A Harriers of VMA-513 on exercise over the Arizona desert. The aircraft are armed with fuel/air explosive tanks on the inner pylons and Zuni rocket pods on the outer pylons. Note that the leading two Harriers are not carrying the Aden gun pods, under-fuselage strakes are carried in their stead. (Rolls-Royce, Bristol)

56. This photograph shows an AV-8A Harrier of VMA-231 engaged in off-base deployment training in April 1980. Note the Zuni rocket pods on the outer pylons and fuel/air explosive tanks on the inner pylons, plus the toned down markings. (R. D. Ward/US DoD)

55▲ 56▼

57. This photograph shows the interim-Sea Control Ship, USS *Guam* (LPH-9) with six AV-8A Harriers of Detachment B of VMA-513 embarked, leaving for trials in the Mediterranean after calling at Southampton in 1972. (BAe Kingston)
58. An AV-8A Harrier, equipped with a flight-refuelling probe, takes-off from the deck of the USS *Guam en route* for the Mediterranean. (BAe Kingston)
59. An AV-8A Harrier of VMA-542 on board HMS *Hermes* in September 1977 during cross-operation exercises in American waters. (Leading Airman (Phot) M. P. McBarron/HMS *Hermes*)

▼59

▲60

60. An AV-8A Harrier of VMA-542 launches a Zuni rocket during weapons trials in Arizona in August 1974. Note the large radio antenna above the wing, a modification peculiar to the AV-8A. (BAe Kingston)

61. Of the USMC requirement for 110 AV-8 Harriers, the last eight aircraft

were ordered as TAV-8A two-seat trainers (T.54). This photograph shows the first TAV-8A at Dunsfold in 1975. These aircraft were all allocated to the Harrier training squadron, VMA(T)-203. (Rolls-Royce, Bristol)

62. A Harrier GR.3 of 1 Squadron firing 68mm air-to-ground rockets from SNEB

pods over the Fenland ranges in England. (BAe Kingston)

63. Another Harrier GR.3 of 1 Squadron, in arctic camouflage with white overpainted on the dark grey, deployed to Tromso airfield in Norway during Exercise 'Anorak Express' in March 1980. (Ian V. Hogg)

▼61

62▲ 63▼

▲64 ▼65

64. Since 1975, the RAF has maintained a detachment of four Harriers in Belize to deter aggression from neighbouring Honduras. The detachment was initially the responsibility of 1 Squadron, although later the OCU took over the task. From 1980, the Belize-based Harriers were designated 1417 Flight, and pilots were detached from the RAF Germany Harrier wing to fly them. This 1981 photograph shows a Harrier GR.3 taxiing to its revetment on the airfield, resplendent in 1417 Flight nose markings. (MoD)

65. Harrier T.4s were retro-fitted with the nose-mounted LRMTS and fin-mounted RWR, as illustrated by this 233 OCU Harrier T.4, with the present nose markings. (MoD/Rep S)

66. Three Sea Harrier FRS.1 aircraft of the Fleet Air Arm, showing the unit markings of the three squadrons in existence prior to the Falklands conflict. Reading from front to back, the aircraft are assigned to 899 Naval Air Squadron (NAS), 800 NAS and 801 NAS. (BAe Kingston)

67. Apart from the USMC, the Spanish Navy also procured the AV-8A version of the Harrier. This photograph shows the single seat AV-8S (as the type was re-designated) to the left, with the two-seat TAV-8S to the right. Both aircraft belong to Escuadrilla 008 and are called 'Matador' in Spanish Navy service. (BAe Kingston)

▲68 ▼69

68. Four Sea Harrier FRS.1 aircraft of 809 NAS during their work-up, prior to deploying to the South Atlantic in April/May 1982. The aircraft are painted in the new air superiority scheme of light aircraft grey overall, with Barley-grey under the wings and tailplane, and they carry toned-down markings. (BAe Kingston)

69. A BAe Sea Harrier FRS.1 of 800 Naval Air Squadron (NAS), armed with two AIM-9L Sidewinder air-to-air missiles (AAMs), takes off from HMS *Hermes* on a combat air patrol mission during the Falklands conflict in 1982. (HMS *Hermes* via BAe Kingston)

70. In 1972, the Spanish Navy ordered six single-seat and two two-seat Harriers, via the US Navy, to operate from their ex-US Navy carrier, *Dedalo*. Virtually identical with the AV-8A, they were designated AV-8S and TAV-8S respectively, and known in Spain as the Matador. This photograph shows the single-seat Matador. (BAe Kingston)

71. An AV-8S Matador of Escuadrilla 008 operating from *Dedalo*, Spain's only aircraft carrier. Later a further four single-seat and one trainer version were ordered, and delivered direct to Spain. (Rolls-Royce, Bristol)

72. One AV-8S Matador lands on *Dedalo*, while a further three Matadors can be seen parked on the starboard side of the ship. (Rolls-Royce, Bristol)

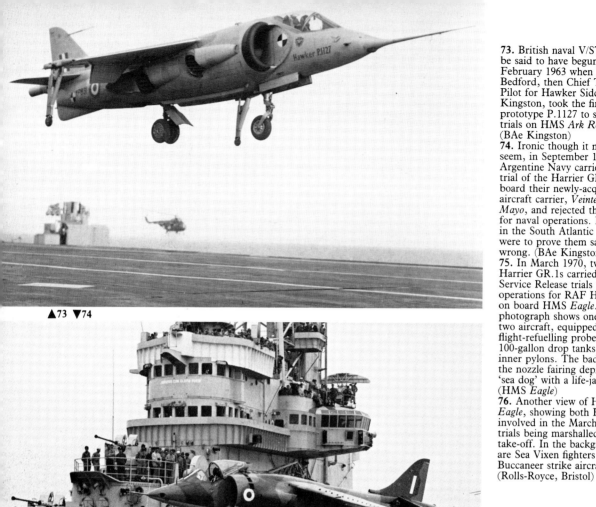

73. British naval V/STOL can be said to have begun in February 1963 when Bill Bedford, then Chief Test Pilot for Hawker Siddeley Kingston, took the first prototype P.1127 to sea for trials on HMS *Ark Royal*. (BAe Kingston)

74. Ironic though it may seem, in September 1969 the Argentine Navy carried out a trial of the Harrier GR.1 on board their newly-acquired aircraft carrier, *Veintecinco de Mayo*, and rejected the type for naval operations. Events in the South Atlantic in 1982 were to prove them sadly wrong. (BAe Kingston)

75. In March 1970, two Harrier GR.1s carried out Service Release trials for deck operations for RAF Harriers on board HMS *Eagle*. This photograph shows one of the two aircraft, equipped with flight-refuelling probe and 100-gallon drop tanks on the inner pylons. The badge on the nozzle fairing depicts a 'sea dog' with a life-jacket! (HMS *Eagle*)

76. Another view of HMS *Eagle*, showing both Harriers involved in the March 1970 trials being marshalled for take-off. In the background are Sea Vixen fighters and Buccaneer strike aircraft. (Rolls-Royce, Bristol)

▲73 ▼74

▼75

76►

77. While a Wessex HAS.3 flies plane guard duties, an RAF Harrier GR.1 makes a short take-off from the angled deck of HMS *Eagle* during the Service Release trials of March 1970. (Rolls-Royce, Bristol)

78. In February 1977, with the impending arrival of Sea Harriers, four Harriers, including G-VTOL, embarked in HMS *Hermes* for a series of trials. This view shows one of the aircraft making a short take-off in heavy weather. Note that the Harrier has been 'zapped' with Royal Navy identification. (HMS *Hermes*)

79. An RAF Harrier T.4 from the Flight Systems Department of RAE Bedford on board HMS *Hermes* during the February 1977 trials. (HMS *Hermes*)

78

79

80. Fitted with specialized equipment necessary for aircraft to operate at night and in poor visibility, this A&AEE Harrier GR.3 lands on *Hermes* during the February 1977 trials. The aircraft is carrying a pair of 100-gallon tanks inboard and a pair of 1,000lb bombs outboard. (HMS *Hermes*)

81. Alongside the development of the Sea Harrier came the discovery that by launching the aircraft from a ramp, soon christened the 'ski-jump', not only could the payload of the aircraft be increased for a given take-off run, but the aircraft could leave the ramp (or ship) in a safer attitude, allowing extra vital seconds for the pilot to eject in the event of an engine failure. This photograph shows a Harrier GR.1 making a test launch from the development ski-jump ramp at RAE Bedford in August 1977. The ramp is set at 6°, and the aircraft is loaded with three 1,000lb bombs. (BAe Kingston)

82. The 500th ski-jump launch from the Bedford ramp, set at 20°, performed by a production Harrier GR.3. The aircraft is carrying a pair of 100-gallon drop tanks and two BL755 cluster bombs. (Peter Hudson, RAE Bedford)

▲80 ▼81

82▶

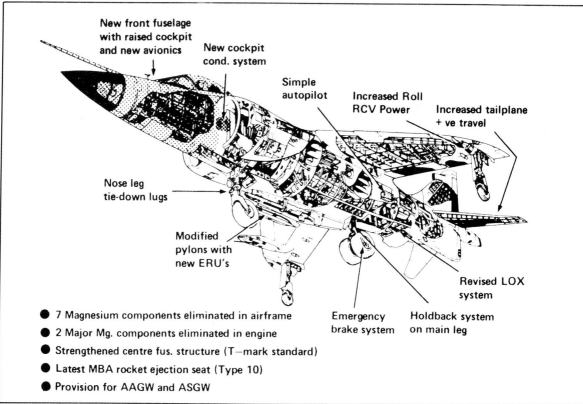

New front fuselage with raised cockpit and new avionics

New cockpit cond. system

Simple autopilot

Increased Roll RCV Power

Increased tailplane + ve travel

Nose leg tie-down lugs

Modified pylons with new ERU's

Revised LOX system

Emergency brake system

Holdback system on main leg

- 7 Magnesium components eliminated in airframe
- 2 Major Mg. components eliminated in engine
- Strengthened centre fus. structure (T–mark standard)
- Latest MBA rocket ejection seat (Type 10)
- Provision for AAGW and ASGW

▲83 ▼84

83. After 12 years of demonstrations, the go-ahead for a maritime Harrier was finally made in May 1975. Developed from the Harrier GR.3, the Sea Harrier FRS.1 was 90 per cent common in airframe and engine, but the avionics were 90 per cent new. This drawing highlights the main changes made for the Sea Harrier. (BAe Kingston)

84. Initial carrier trials were carried out by 700A NAS on board HMS *Hermes* in October 1979, when two of their aircraft joined two A&AEE Boscombe Down Sea Harriers and one development aircraft from BAe Dunsfold. Three of those Sea Harriers are shown here. (Leading Airman D. du Feu, HMS *Hermes*)

85. The first Sea Harrier first flew in August 1978, and in September 1979 the Navy's Intensive Flying Trials Unit, 700A NAS, was commissioned. This photograph shows one of 700A's aircraft at RNAS Yeovilton. Note the raised cockpit and bulged canopy, plus the radar nose. (MJG)

86. The discovery of the benefits of ski-jump ramps made modifications to the Royal Navy's new *Invincible* class of ASW carrier necessary. The first two ships, *Invincible* and *Illustrious* have 6½° ramps, while the third, *Ark Royal*, will have a 12° ramp. HMS *Hermes* was also fitted with a 12° ramp. This photograph shows the first Sea Harrier ski-jump launch at sea from HMS *Invincible* on 30 October 1980. (HMS *Invincible*)

87. A Sea Harrier FRS.1, equipped with twin 30mm Aden cannon, two 100-gallon drop tanks and a pair of AIM-9 Sidewinder AAMs, lands on board *Hermes* during the October 1979 trials. In the foreground is the tail of another Sea Harrier, showing the rear RWR antenna and fin RWR antenna to advantage. (HMS *Hermes*)

88. A Sea Harrier FRS.1 of 700A NAS flies over the Somerset countryside close to its shore base of Yeovilton. Note the long Pitot tube reaching forward of the nose radome. (HMS *Heron*)

89. A sight many people never expected to see. HMS *Hermes* leaves Portsmouth Harbour on 5 April 1982 as flagship of the British Task Force which was to re-take the Falkland Islands from the Argentine invaders. Eight 800 and 899 NAS Sea Harriers were augmented by a further three from service research and development establishments. The 12° ski-jump is clearly visible on the forward flight deck. (HMS *Hermes*)

90. This artist's impression shows the novel concept, proposed by Vosper Thornycroft in 1976, of a small 'Harrier Carrier' capable of operating eight Sea Harriers and a pair of SAR helicopters. The flight deck has a built-in ski-jump curve at the bow. The 'Harrier Carrier' has, however, remained something of a pipedream. (Vosper Thornycroft)

▲87 ▼88

89▲ 90▼

▲91

91. The Fleet Air Arm's first operational Sea Harrier unit was 800 NAS, which commissioned in April 1980. This photograph shows one of 800's aircraft at that time, resplendent in dark sea-grey and white finish, with 'D'-type roundels and colourful squadron insignia on the tail. (HMS *Heron*)

92. The second Sea Harrier unit, 801 NAS was commissioned in January 1981 and would be deployed on board *Invincible*. Like her 800 NAS colleague,

this Sea Harrier is in her pre-Falklands colour scheme. Note that the fuselage strakes are fitted in place of the gun pods under the fuselage, and that three CBLS are carried in addition to the 100-gallon drop tanks. (Nigel B. Thomas/801 NAS)

93. Flying above Dartmouth Harbour, with the Royal Yacht *Britannia* at anchor, are three Sea Harriers representing the three pre-Falklands units. Leading the formation is an aircraft of 899 NAS (HQ unit, OCU and

reserve squadron), 801 NAS (HMS *Invincible*), and 800 NAS (HMS *Hermes*). (BAe Kingston)

94. Prior to development of the Sea Eagle, development trials were carried out with the HSD/Matra AS.37 Martel anti-radiation missile. This photograph shows XV277 with a Martel under each inboard pylon. In the event, this missile type was only operationally deployed on Buccaneer strike aircraft. (BAe Kingston)

▼92

93▲ 94▼

▲95

95. A Sea Harrier FRS.1 from A&AEE Boscombe Down, seen on a test flight carrying a pair of BAeD Sea Eagle sea-skimming anti-ship missiles now under development for use by RAF Buccaneers and Tornados, and the Sea Harrier. Sea Eagle should be in service by 1985, and is credited with a range of between 50km and 100km. (BAe Kingston)

96. The Falklands conflict changed the colour schemes applied to the Fleet Air Arm's Sea Harriers. This photograph, taken aboard HMS *Hermes* during her voyage to the South Atlantic shows the old (to the rear) and the new. The white undersides of the aircraft were painted dark sea-grey to match the upper surfaces, all colourful squadron markings were painted out, and the 'D'-type roundels had their white band over-painted with blue, to make a disproportionate 'B'-type roundel. (BAe Kingston)

97. This 800 NAS Sea Harrier, armed with gun pods, underwing tanks and a pair of AIM-9L Sidewinder AAMs, is being marshalled to the take-off point on *Hermes* during the Falklands conflict. Revised figures issued by the UK MoD in their White Paper on the lessons of the Falklands Campaign, credit AIM-9 Sidewinders with 16 kills and one probable. (HMS *Hermes* via MoD)

98. Definitely off Ascension Island, this view shows all eight 809 NAS Sea Harriers, plus six RAF Harrier GR.3s, on board the ill-fated *Atlantic Conveyor*. The patch-type markings on the outer wings of the Harrier GR.3s probably indicate where holes were made to gain access to the wing while installing wiring to enable the GR.3 to be equipped with AIM-9 Sidewinder AAMs. Note also the Chinook and Wessex helicopters, which are still wrapped in their protective cocoons. (Via BAe Kingston)

99. After the Task Force had set sail, the Fleet Air Arm gathered together a further eight Sea Harriers, and in April 1982 reformed 809 NAS as the reinforcement squadron for deployment in the South Atlantic. The aircraft were finished in a camouflage scheme adapted from RAF Phantoms, of medium sea-grey overall, with Barley-grey (named after Mr Barley of RAE Farnborough, who developed the colour) on the underside of the wings and tailplane. This 809 NAS aircraft is seen on the landing pad of the *Atlantic Conveyor*, probably while at anchor off Ascension Island. (Via BAe Kingston)

100. The first of six Sea Harrier FRS.51 for the Indian Navy seen during trials in summer 1982. The first aircraft for 300 Squadron of the Indian Fleet Air Arm was handed over on 26 January 1983. (BAe Kingston)

101. This line-up of Harriers at the US Navy Test Centre at Patuxent River shows the two prototype YAV-8Bs tucked between a pair of AV-8As and a VMA(T)-203 TAV-8A in April 1979. (McDonnell Douglas)

▲98 ▼99

▲102

▲103 ▼104

102. One of the four full-scale development (FSD) McDonnell Douglas AV-8B Harrier II trials aircraft carrying 16 Mk.82 570lb bombs during trials from the US Navy Test Centre at Patuxent River in Maryland. (McDonnell Douglas)

103. The first McDonnell Douglas AV-8B full-scale development (FSD) aircraft on its maiden flight on 5 November 1981. Flown by project test pilot Charles Summers, the AV-8B made five vertical take-offs and hovers which amounted to 12 minutes air time. The next day, the aircraft made a conventional flight from St. Louis. Note the raised canopy, underside LIDs and large wing flaps. (McDonnell Douglas)

104. The fourth FSD Harrier II is now flying in an experimental air superiority scheme of three shades of grey. The toned-down national insignia can just be seen on the front nozzle fairing. (McDonnell Douglas)

105. While the Fleet Air Arm were busy preparing 809 NAS, the RAF were equally busy modifying their Harrier GR.3s to carry and fight with AIM-9 Sidewinder AAMs. This view shows one such aircraft during the system clearance trials at RAF Wittering during April 1982. (RAF Wittering)

106. Another system used with success during the Falklands campaign was the Paveway II laser-guided bomb (LGB). Two raids were carried out with this weapon on the closing days of the conflict (13 and 14 June). The Paveway II LGB can be seen on the outer pylons of the Harrier GR.3 in the foreground of this line-up of Harriers and Sea Harriers aboard *Hermes*. (HMS *Hermes* via RAF Wittering)

105▲ 106▼

◄104

107. An RAF Harrier GR.3 prepares to launch off the ski-jump ramp on *Hermes* during one of the early raids, after their arrival with the Task Force in May 1982. The aircraft is armed with the two gun pods, two 100-gallon underwing tanks and three BL755 cluster bombs (CBUs). (HMS *Hermes* via RAF Wittering)

108. This photograph shows a Sea Harrier about to make a short take-off from the forward operating base set up at Port San Carlos. Another Sea Harrier and two Harrier GR.3s can be seen in the background. (Via BAe Kingston)

109. A Harrier GR.3 of 1 Squadron, armed with the 2in rocket pods, taxies on aluminium planking at the forward operating base at Port San Carlos during the Falklands campaign. (Via RAF Wittering)

▲107 ▼108

▲110

110. An 809 NAS Sea Harrier FRS.1
armed with guns and Sidewinders seen
against the bleak terrain of the
Falklands. It is thought that this aircraft
was one of the two which transferred
direct from HMS *Invincible* to HMS
Illustrious on the latter's arrival in the
South Atlantic in August 1982. (Via BAe
Kingston)

111. Following the re-capture of the
Falkland Islands, the RAF retains a
number of Harrier GR.3s there, to
supplement the Phantoms flown in after
the runway of Port Stanley had been
repaired and lengthened. As this
photograph shows, 1 Sqn retain their
AIM-9 Sidewinder capability. The
aircraft is parked on aluminium matting,
and the conditions in which the two
groundcrew are working on the aircraft
are typical. (Richard E. Gardner)

▼111

112. During the summer of 1982, Sea Harriers returning from the Falklands were given major services and many were re-painted in the medium sea-grey and Barley-grey scheme. Initially the first aircraft were assigned to 809 NAS to equip the air group on board HMS *Illustrious* heading south to relieve HMS *Invincible*. Others were assigned to 899 NAS, the HQ unit at Yeovilton. This particular aircraft is an 899 NAS

machine, but note the standard colours for the fuselage roundel, rather than the pale colours that go with this style. (MJG)

113. Until the arrival of the RAF Phantoms, air defence was the main responsibility of Sea Harriers from, initially, HMS *Invincible*, and later HMS *Illustrious*. Here is ZA194/251 of 809 NAS, the penultimate Sea Harrier (before extra aircraft were ordered)

waiting on quick reaction alert at Port Stanley airfield. Deployed ashore from *Illustrious*, the aircraft is equipped with the larger 190-gallon underwing tanks and twin Sidewinder launchers, developed in response to operational needs in the South Atlantic. (Richard E. Gardner)

115▲

◀114

114. Following the
experiences of two major
types of colour scheme in
combat, it has been decided
to repaint the Sea Harriers in
an overall dark sea-grey
scheme, with standard
'B'-type roundels, as
illustrated here. The aircraft
banking away clearly shows
the 190-gallon underwing fuel
tanks mentioned earlier.
(Nigel B. Thomas/HMS
Heron)
115. This view shows
ZA455/000 of 801 NAS on
arrival back at Yeovilton in
September 1982, after
disembarking from *Invincible*.
During the conflict,
Invincible's Sea Harriers were
known as 'The Black Death'
by Argentine pilots they
encountered in combat.
(R. L. Ward)

▲116

116. The latest scheme for Sea Harriers is illustrated by this 800 NAS aircraft, deployed on board HMS *Hermes*. This particular aircraft appears to have retained the modified 'D' to 'B'-type roundels. (800 NAS via R. L. Ward)

117. This view shows a Rolls-Royce development Harrier GR.3 (XV277) fitted with zero-scarf form nozzles. The term 'scarf' comes from carpentry, and refers to the angle of cutaway of the nozzle. Zero-scarf means that the nozzle is not cut back, so as to direct the efflux of the jet more efficiently in the ground effect. An additional advantage is that zero-scarf nozzles offer

extra thrust, in the region of 200lb. (Rolls-Royce, Bristol)

118. The Indian Navy was the first export customer for the Sea Harrier, and six FRS.51 aircraft are on order. The first of these was handed over on 27 January 1983 at BAe's Dunsfold factory. Initially, the Indian Navy Sea Harriers will be based at Yeovilton in the UK, as their pilots and instructors are trained. By mid-summer 1983, the first Sea Harriers will be flying from INS *Vikrant*. This photo shows John Farley making his famed 'Farley take-off' during the Farnborough Air Show 1982, in the first Indian Sea Harrier. (BAe Kingston)

▼117 118▶

▲119 ▼120

119. During the mid-1970s, British Aerospace (Hawker Siddeley as it then was) and McDonnell Douglas were collaborating on a follow-up for the AV-8A Harrier, with roughly twice the speed and performance of the AV-8A, designated AV-16. This aircraft was to be offered to the USMC, US Navy, RAF and Fleet Air Arm. As this artist's impression shows, the resulting design is not dissimilar to a stretched Sea Harrier with a new wing. (BAe via Bill Gunston)

120. Following the demise of the studies between the UK and the United States on a Harrier/AV-8A replacement, known as the AV-16, the USMC still wished for a follow-on aircraft. McDonnell Douglas received a contract in October 1976 to modify two existing AV-8A Harriers to an improved YAV-8B configuration. This involved fitting a new supercritical wing (of composite construction), larger air intakes, lift improvement devices (LIDs) and fitting a zero-scarf nozzle to the front pair of Pegasus engine vectored-thrust exhausts. The first aircraft, seen here with a standard AV-8A (in camouflage) for comparison, made its first flight on 9 November 1978. Note the strakes on the underside of the gun pods: these are part of the LIDs. (McDonnell Douglas)

121. This photograph shows the second prototype YAV-8B armed with the gun pod, seven Mk 82 bombs and a pair of AIM-9L Sidewinder AAMs. Both YAV-8Bs are powered by Rolls-Royce Pegasus 11 turbofans, delivering 21,500lb of thrust, and the aircraft can carry 9,000lb of underwing stores. (McDonnell Douglas)

122. This underside view of the AV-8B clearly shows the LIDs, including the 'dam' which is lowered between the gun pod/strake position, the large flaps and the airbrake. Note also the zero-scarf nozzles on the front pair of exhausts and the double row of blow-in doors on the side of the air intake. (Rolls-Royce, Bristol)

121▲ 122▼

67

123. In June 1982, the second prototype YAV-8B made a series of tests at Edwards AFB in California. For these tests the aircraft was repainted in a red, black, gold and white colour scheme, so that the positions of control surfaces and aircraft attitudes could be clearly distinguished during the tests. (McDonnell Douglas)

▲124 ▼125

126▲ 127▼

124. During 1978, the RAF split their Air Staff Target (AST) 403 for a Harrier and Jaguar replacement into AST 403 for the Jaguar and ASR (Requirement replacing Target in the acronym) 409 for a Harrier replacement. This model illustrates BAe Kingston's submission for a 'Big Wing' Harrier retrofit, complete with leading edge root extensions (LERX) for improved manoeuvrability. Up to 100 aircraft to this configuration would have been produced, partly by retro-fitting some GR.3s. (BAe Kingston)

125. In the event, however, ASR 409 was met by a slightly modified AV-8B, fitted with LERX and other small equipment changes. McDonnell Douglas concluded a 60:40 per cent co-production deal with British Aerospace for the airframe production, while the Rolls-Royce and Pratt & Whitney deal for the Pegasus engine is roughly 75:25 per cent. The RAF are to receive 60 AV-8Bs, redesignated Harrier GR.5. Deliveries to the RAF from the Kingston/Dunsfold production line are expected from mid-1986. This model shows a GR.5 in 4 Squadron markings. RAF GR.5s will replace GR.3s in the two German-based squadrons. (BAe Kingston)

126. The third FSD AV-8B here shows off its LERX and the raised canopy. The USMC are to receive 336 AV-8B Harrier IIs (plus the four FSD aircraft) to replace three AV-8A/C squadrons and five A-4M Skyhawk squadrons, both deliveries beginning from October 1983. (McDonnell Douglas)

127. Developed in parallel with the YAV-8B was an update programme for the AV-8A, to enable the remaining USMC aircraft to operate effectively until the AV-8B enters service. Designated AV-8C, the update takes the form of a CILOP (Conversion In Lieu Of Procurement) programme which adds internal RWR, improved UHF communications, chaff/flare dispensers, an OBOGS (On-Board Oxygen Generating System), secure voice links and the AV-8B pod strakes and 'dam'. Shown here is the development AV-8C. (McDonnell Douglas)

128. And for the future . . . McDonnell Douglas and Rolls-Royce are proposing a flight-test demonstrator for a Mach 1.6 supersonic V/STOL programme. An AV-8A airframe would be modified to AV-8SX configuration as shown in this artist's impression, while the Pegasus 11 turbofan would have PCB added to the front nozzles. (McDonnell Douglas)

128▼

129. It was originally proposed that the USMC procure a further batch of TAV-8A Harrier trainers from British Aerospace to support the AV-8B training programme. However, following pressure from the US General Accounting Office, it now looks as if a TAV-8B will be built. This model illustrates how the TAV-8B would look, and deliveries could begin in 1985. (McDonnell Douglas)

130. Again for the future . . . BAe Kingston's approach to supersonic STOVL can be seen in the form of the P.1214–3 (now known as the P.1216), a forward-swept twin-tail aircraft with a lobster-back version of the Pegasus. The twin front vectored-thrust nozzles would have PCB, as would the single 'lobster-back' rear nozzle, positioned below the fuselage. (BAe Kingston)

▼129

▼130